NIETZSCHE IN 90 MINUTES

DEC 05

DISCARD

WESTMINSTER PUBLIC LIBRARY
3031 WEST 76th AVE.
WESTMINSTER, CO 80030

Nietzsche
IN 90 MINUTES

Paul Strathern

IVAN R. DEE
CHICAGO

WESTMINSTER PUBLIC LIBRARY
3031 WEST 76th AVE.
WESTMINSTER, CO 80030

NIETZSCHE IN 90 MINUTES. Copyright © 1996 by Paul
Strathern. All rights reserved, including the right to reproduce
this book or portions thereof in any form. For information,
address: Ivan R. Dee, Inc., 1332 North Halsted Street, Chicago
60622. Manufactured in the United States of America and
printed on acid-free paper.

Library of Congress Cataloging-in-Publication Data:
Strathern, Paul, 1940–
    Nietzsche in 90 minutes / Paul Strathern.
      p.   cm. — (Philosophers in 90 minutes)
    Includes bibliographical references and index.
    ISBN 1-56663-120-3 (cloth : alk. paper). —
    ISBN 1-56663-121-1 (paper : alk. paper)
    1. Nietzsche, Friedrich Wilhelm, 1844–1900.   I. Title.
II. Series.
B3317.S73   1996
193—dc20   96-28105

Contents

NIETZSCHE IN 90 MINUTES

Introduction

Early in the Christian era, philosophy fell asleep. These slumbers eventually produced the philosophic dream known as Scholasticism, based on Aristotle and the teachings of the church.

Philosophy was rudely awakened from these medieval slumbers in the seventeenth century by the arrival of Descartes, with his declaration "Cogito ergo sum" (I think, therefore I am). An age of enlightenment had begun: knowledge was based on reason. But Descartes woke up more than the sleeping scholars. He also woke up the British. They soon responded to Descartes's rational claim by insisting that our knowledge is not based on reason but on experience. In their zeal, these British empiricists soon destroyed all semblance of reason—reducing philosophy to a series of ever-diminishing sensations. Philosophy was in danger of going to sleep again. Then, in the middle of the eighteenth century, Kant awoke from his dogmatic slumbers and produced an even greater philosophical system than the one which had put philosophy to sleep throughout the Middle Ages. It looked as if philosophy would once again soon be emulating Rip van Winkle. Hegel reacted to this soporific situation by constructing a huge systematic four-poster bed of his own. Schopenhauer decided to try a different tack and introduced a draft of chilly oriental philosophy into the Kantian bed. This had the effect of waking up the young Nietzsche, who leaped into the icy blast and began proclaiming a loud philosophy that was to keep everyone awake for a long time to come.

Nietzsche's Life and Works

With Nietzsche philosophy becomes dangerous again, this time with a difference. In previous centuries philosophy had been dangerous for philosophers; with Nietzsche it becomes dangerous for everyone. Nietzsche ended up by going mad, and this begins to show in the tone of his later writings. But the dangerous ideas started appearing long before he went mad, and have nothing to do with clinical insanity. They presaged a collective madness which was to have horrific consequences in Europe during the first half of the twentieth century, and which shows ominous signs of recurrence today.

Nietzsche's larger philosophical ideas are

barely worthy of the name—whether he's talking about supermen, eternal recurrence (the idea that we live our lives again and again throughout eternity), or the sole purpose of civilization (to produce "great men" such as Goethe, Napoleon, and himself). His use of the Will to Power as a universal explanation is either simplistic or meaningless—even Freud's monism is more subtle, and Schopenhauer's less specific concept is more convincing. Like any good conspiracy theory, Nietzsche's doctrine of the all-pervasive Will to Power contains the usual element of paranoia. But Nietzsche's actual philosophizing is as brilliant, persuasive, and incisive as any before or since. When reading him you get the exhilarating feeling that philosophy actually matters (which is one of the reasons why he is so dangerous). And when he used the Will to Power purely as an analytic tool, it enabled him to discover constituent elements in human motives which few had formerly suspected. This allowed him to unmask the values to which these motives gave rise, and trace the development of these values over a broad historical canvas, illuminating the very foundations of our civilization and culture.

Although Nietzsche is not entirely free from blame for the dangerous nonsense that has been spouted in his name, it must be said that most of this is a travesty of what he actually wrote. He had nothing but contempt for the protofascists of his era, anti-Semitism disgusted him, and the idea of a nation of racially pure Germans becoming a master race would certainly have exercised his sense of humor to the full. Had he lived (and retained his sanity) until the 1930s, when he would have been in his eighties, he would certainly not have remained silent about the grotesque events taking place in his homeland—like some German philosophers of that era who claimed to be his successors.

Friedrich Wilhelm Nietzsche was born October 15, 1844, in Saxony, which was by this time a province of the increasingly powerful kingdom of Prussia. Nietzsche was descended from a long line of tradesmen, including hatters and butchers, but his grandfather and father were both

Lutheran pastors. Nietzsche's father was a patriotic Prussian who held his king, Friedrich Wilhelm IV, in high esteem. When Ludwig Nietzsche's first son was born on the king's birthday, it was obvious that he had little chance of being named Otto. By an utterly meaningless coincidence, all three men were to die insane.

The first to go was Ludwig, who died in 1849. He was diagnosed as having "softening of the brain"—and the autopsy apparently revealed that a quarter of his brain had been affected by "softening." This diagnosis is no longer fashionable with the medical profession, but Nietzsche's reputable biographers are convinced that Ludwig Nietzsche's insanity was not inherited by his son.

Nietzsche was now brought up in Naumburg in a house full of "holy women," which included a mother, a younger sister, a maternal grandmother, and two slightly loopy maiden aunts. This appears to have affected Nietzsche's attitude toward women in later life. At the age of thirteen he went to boarding school at nearby Pforta, one of the top private boarding schools in Germany. Nietzsche, very much the product of his pious, mollycoddled upbringing, became known as "the little pastor" and carried off all the prizes. But he was so brilliant that eventually he couldn't help thinking for himself. By the age of eighteen he was beginning to doubt his faith. The clear-sighted thinker couldn't help noticing the square pegs in the round holes of the world about him. Typically this thinking appears to have been done in complete isolation. Throughout his life Nietzsche was to be influenced in his thought by very few living people (and not many dead ones either).

At the age of nineteen Nietzsche went to the University of Bonn to study theology and classical philology, with the aim of becoming a pastor. His destiny had been mapped out long beforehand by the "holy women"; but already he was beginning to experience an unconscious urge to rebellion, which resulted in a transformation of his character. On arriving at Bonn the solitary schoolboy unexpectedly became a typical gregarious student. He joined a smart fraternity, took to drinking with his fellows, and even fought a duel (the usual artificial affair, which was stopped as soon as he had received his honorable scar—a slight nick on the nose, unfortunately later obscured by the bridge of his spectacles). But this was only a necessary phase. By now Nietzsche had decided "God is dead." (This remark, now so closely associated with Nietzsche and his philosophy, was also made by Hegel some twenty years before Nietzsche was born.) At home during the holidays he refused to take communion and announced that he would not be entering the church. The next year he decided to switch to Leipzig University, where he would drop theology and concentrate on classical philology.

Nietzsche arrived in Leipzig in October 1865, in the same month that he celebrated his twenty-first birthday. Around this time two events took place which were to transform his life. While on a sight-seeing trip to Cologne, he visited a brothel. According to Nietzsche this visit was inadvertent. On arrival he had asked a street porter to lead him to a restaurant; instead the porter took him to a brothel. The way Nietzsche later related it to a friend: "All at once I found myself surrounded by half a dozen apparitions in tinsel and gauze, gazing at me expectantly. For a brief moment I was speechless. Then I made instinctively for the only soulful thing present in the place: the piano. I played a few chords, which freed me from my paralysis, and I escaped."

Inevitably we only have Nietzsche's evidence regarding this unlikely episode. Whether or not the visit was quite so accidental, and whether or not Nietzsche ended up only fondling the keys of the piano, it is impossible to tell. Nietzsche was almost certainly still a virgin at the time. He was an extremely intense young man as well as being inexperienced and gauche in the ways of the world. (Yet this didn't stop him from making pronouncements about such matters. Despite his sexual status, he earnestly informed a friend that he would need to keep three women to satisfy him.)

On later consideration Nietzsche must have decided that he had been attracted by something more than the piano. He went back to the brothel and almost certainly paid a few visits to similar establishments when he returned to Leipzig. Not long after this he discovered that he was infected. The doctor who treated him wouldn't have told him that he had syphilis (they didn't in those days, because it was incurable). Even so, as a result of this incident Nietzsche appears to have abstained from sexual activity with women. Despite this he continued throughout his life to make embarrassingly self-revealing remarks about them in his philosophy. "You are going to see a woman? Do not forget your whip." (Although it's possible that, owing to the type of bordello he had visited in Leipzig, he thought it only fair that men should be equally armed for the fray.)

The second life-changing incident took place when he entered a secondhand bookshop and came across a copy of Schopenhauer's *The World as Will and Representation*. "I took the unfamiliar book in my hands and began leafing through the pages. I don't know what demon it was that whispered in my ear: 'Take this book home.' So, breaking my principle of never buying a book too quickly, I did just that. Back home I threw myself into the corner of the sofa with my new treasure, and began to let that dynamic gloomy genius work on my mind. . . . I found myself looking into a mirror which reflected the world, life and my own nature with terrifying grandeur. . . . Here I saw sickness and health, exile and refuge, Hell and Heaven."

As a result of these astonishingly prophetic sentiments, Nietzsche became a Schopenhauerian. At this time, when Nietzsche had nothing to believe in, he needed Schopenhauer's pessimism and detachment. According to Schopenhauer, the world is merely representation, supported by an all-pervasive evil will. This will is blind and pays no attention to the concerns of mere humanity, inflicting upon its members a life of suffering as they strive against its manifestation all around them (the world). Our only sensible course is to lessen the power of the will within us by living a life of renunciation and asceticism.

Schopenhauer's pessimism didn't quite fit Nietzsche's nature, but he at once recognized its honesty and power. From now on his positive

17

ideas would first have to be of sufficient strength to go beyond this pessimism. The way forward lay through Schopenhauer. But most of all, Schopenhauer's concept of the fundamental role played by the will was to prove decisive. This was eventually to become transformed into Nietzsche's Will to Power.

In 1867 Nietzsche was called up for a year's national service in the Prussian army. The authorities were obviously fooled by the large and ferocious military mustache that Nietzsche had now cultivated beneath his rather disappointing dueling scar, and he was dispatched to the cavalry. This was a mistake. Nietzsche had great determination but a pitifully frail physique. He suffered a serious riding accident and then rode on as if nothing had happened, in the best Prussian tradition. When Private Nietzsche made it back to barracks he had to be hospitalized for a month. He was promoted to lance corporal for effort, and then sent home.

Back at Leipzig University, Nietzsche was now recognized by his professor as the finest student he had seen in forty years. Yet Nietzsche was becoming disenchanted with philology and its "indifference towards the true and urgent problems of life." He didn't know what to do. In desperation he thought of switching to chemistry, or going off to Paris for a year to try "the divine cancan and the yellow poison absinthe." Then one day he managed to secure an introduction to the composer Richard Wagner, who was on an undercover visit to the city. (Wagner had been banished for revolutionary activities twenty years earlier, and the ban remained despite the transformation of his extremist political views from left to right.)

Wagner had been born in the same year as Nietzsche's father and from all accounts bore a striking resemblance to him. Nietzsche felt a desperate—but largely unconscious—need for a father figure. He had never met a famous artist before, nor someone whose ideas were apparently so in accord with his own. In the course of their brief meeting Nietzsche discovered Wagner's deep love of Schopenhauer. Wagner, flattered by the attentions of the brilliant young philosopher, turned on his considerable charm to

19

the full. The effect on Nietzsche was immediate and profound. He was overwhelmed by the great composer, whose flamboyant character was at least the equal of his flamboyant operas.

Two months later Nietzsche was offered the post of professor of philology at the University of Basel in Switzerland. He was still only twenty-four and had not yet even taken his doctorate. Despite his misgivings about philology, this was an offer he could not refuse. In April 1869 he took up his post at Basel and at once began giving extra lectures in philosophy. He wished to combine philosophy and philology, the study of aesthetics and the classics—welding together an instrument for analyzing the faults of our civilization, no less. He quickly established himself as the rising young star of the university and became acquainted with Jacob Burckhardt, the great cultural historian who was also a member of the university faculty. Burckhardt, who was the first to elaborate the historical concept of the Renaissance, was the only mind of a caliber similar to Nietzsche's among the faculty, and perhaps the only figure Nietzsche was to remain in awe of throughout his life. It's possible that Burckhardt might, at this crucial stage, have exercised a steadying influence on Nietzsche, but his patrician reserve was to prevent this. And besides, the role of father figure had already been taken—by a far less steadying influence.

In Basel Nietzsche was only forty miles from Tribschen, where Wagner had taken up residence with Cosima, Liszt's daughter (who was at the time still married to a mutual friend of Liszt and Wagner, the conductor von Bülow). In no time Nietzsche became a regular weekend visitor to Wagner's sumptuous villa on the shores of Lake Lucerne. But Wagner's life was operatic in more than just musical, emotional, and political terms. He was a man who believed in living out his fantasies to the full. Tribschen was like an opera in itself, and there was never any doubt about who was playing the leading role. Dressed in the "Flemish style" (a blend of the Flying Dutchman and Rubens in fancy dress), Wagner strode beneath the pink satin walls and rococo cherubs in his black satin breeches, tam-o'-shanter, and effusively knotted silk cravat, declaiming among

21

the busts of himself, vast oil paintings (of the same subject), and silver bowls commemorating performances of his operas. Incense wafted through the air, and only the music of the maestro was allowed to waft with it. Meanwhile Cosima ministered to her companion's histrionics and made sure no one ran off with the perfumed pet lambs, beribboned wolfhounds, and ornamental chickens that roamed the garden.

It's difficult to understand how Nietzsche was taken in by all this. Indeed, it's difficult to understand how anyone was taken in by it. (Wagner's extravagances left him constantly broke, and he relied on support from a string of rich benefactors, including King Ludwig of Bavaria who contributed heavily from the state exchequer.) Only when one listens to Wagner's music does the deep persuasiveness and fatal charm of his character become conceivable. The composer himself was evidently as overwhelming as his spellbinding compositions. The immature Nietzsche quickly fell under the spell of this heady atmosphere, where leitmotifs of unconscious fantasy permeated the rococo salons.

Wagner may have been Dad, but Nietzsche soon found he had an oedipal itch for Cosima. Without daring to declare it (even to himself), he fell in love with her.

In July 1870 the Franco-Prussian War broke out. This was Prussia's chance to avenge its defeat by Napoleon, its opportunity to conquer the French and establish Germany as the major power in Europe. Filled with patriotic fervor, Nietzsche volunteered for service as a medical orderly. Passing through Frankfurt on his way to the front, he witnessed the lines of cavalry clattering through the streets in full regalia. It was as if a scale fell from his eyes. "I felt for the first time that the strongest and highest Will to Life is not to be found in the struggle for existence, but in a Will to Power, a will to war and domination." The Will to Power had been born, and though it was to go through considerable modification, eventually being seen in individual and social rather than purely military terms, it was never to break quite free from its original military inspiration.

Meanwhile, as Bismarck crushed the French,

Nietzsche was to discover that war was not all glory. On the battlefield at Wörth he found himself working amidst a scene "bespattered everywhere with human remains and reeking pungently of corpses." Later he was put into a cattle truck to tend six wounded men on a journey which lasted over two days. Locked in among the shattered bones, gangrenous flesh, and dying soldiers, Nietzsche manfully did his best—but by the time they arrived at Karlsruhe he was a broken man himself. He was shipped to hospital suffering from dysentery and diphtheria.

Despite this traumatic experience, within two months Nietzsche was back teaching in Basel. He continued to overload himself with lectures in philosophy as well as philology, and began writing *The Birth of Tragedy*. This brilliant and highly original analysis of Greek culture contrasts the clear-cut Apollonian element of classical restraint with the darker, instinctual Dionysian forces. According to Nietzsche, the great art of Greek tragedy came from a fusion of these two elements, which was eventually destroyed by the shallow rationalism of Socrates. This was the first time the darker element of Greek culture had been emphasized, and Nietzsche's characterization of it as fundamental proved highly controversial. During the nineteenth century the classical world was sacred. Its ideals of justice, culture, and democracy appealed to the self-image of the emerging middle classes. No one wanted to hear that this had all been a big mistake. Even more controversial was Nietzsche's frequent use of Wagner and his "music of the future" to illustrate his philosophical arguments. Indeed, he wrote to his publisher: "The real aim [of this book] is to illuminate Richard Wagner, that extraordinary enigma of our time, in his relation to Greek tragedy." Only Wagner managed to combine both the Apollonian and Dionysian elements in the manner of Greek tragedy.

This emphasis on the power-filled Dionysian element was to prove an essential part of Nietzsche's later philosophy. No longer could he condone Schopenhauer's "Buddhistic negation of the Will." Instead he pitted this Dionysian element against the Christian elements that he considered to have weakened civilization. He understood that most of our impulses are double-edged. Even our so-called better impulses have their dark or degenerate side: "Every ideal presupposes love and hate, reverence and contempt. The essential impulse can arise from either the positive or negative side." In his view Christianity started from the negative. It had taken hold in the Roman Empire as the religion of the oppressed and slaves. This was everywhere evident in its attitude to life. It constantly sought to overcome our more powerful positive instincts. This negation was both conscious (in the espousal of asceticism and self-denial) and unconscious (with regard to meekness, which he saw as an unconscious expression of resentment, an inversion of aggression by the weak).

Likewise Nietzsche attacked compassion, the repression of true feelings and the sublimation of desire involved in Christianity, in favor of a stronger ethic closer to the origins of our feelings. God was dead, the Christian era was finished. At its worst the twentieth century proved him right; at its best it showed that many of the better "Christian" elements do not depend upon a belief in God. Whether or not we now live closer to our basic feelings remains debatable.

Wagner was a supreme artist, but he was not up to philosophical thinking of this order. Gradually Nietzsche began to see through Wagner's intellectual disguise. Wagner was a walking ego, of great size and intuitive power—but even his love of Schopenhauer was a passing phase, just grist to the mill for his art. Previously Nietzsche had been willing to overlook certain nastier elements in the Wagner household, such as his anti-Semitism, his overweening arrogance, and his unwillingness to recognize the ability or needs of anyone other than himself. But there were limits. By now Wagner had moved to Bayreuth, where King Ludwig of Bavaria was building him a theatre which would be devoted exclusively to the performance of his operas (a project which was to help bankrupt the Bavarian exchequer and contribute to Ludwig being deposed). In 1876 Nietzsche arrived at Bayreuth for the opening performance of Wagner's Ring cycle but fell ill, almost certainly from psychosomatic causes. The megalomania and high art decadence had all become too much for him, and he had to leave.

Two years later Nietzsche published his collection of aphorisms *Human, All Too Human*, which completed the break with Wagner. Nietzsche's praise of French art, his psychological acumen and deflation of romantic pretensions, and his sheer perceptiveness were all too much for Wagner. Worse still, the work contained no unsolicited advertisements for "the music of the future."

Perhaps more important, this work also succeeded in alienating some of Nietzsche's more genuine philosophical admirers. Ironically the cause of this was the one reason he is now universally admired (even by those who abhor his philosophy). In this work Nietzsche began evolving the style that enabled him to become a master of the German language. (No mean task this, with a language such as German—one which has defeated even some of its most esteemed writers.) Nietzsche's style had always been clear and combative, his ideas concentrated yet immediately comprehensible. But now he took to writing in aphorisms. Rather than using long-winded argument, he preferred to present his ideas in a series of penetrating insights, swiftly passing from topic to topic.

Nietzsche philosophized on the hoof in more ways than one. His best ideas came to him during long walks in the Swiss countryside. He frequently claimed to have been out walking for longer than three hours, despite his frail health (though this could well be a projection of the Will to Power, rather than an actual manifestation of it). It has even been claimed that Nietzsche's aphoristic style resulted from his habit of jotting down his thoughts in a notebook while he was on the move. Whatever the cause, this aphoristic habit of Nietzsche's was to result in a style unparalleled throughout Europe during the nineteenth century. This is a large claim (though Nietzsche would certainly have agreed with it). The nineteenth century was an age of great stylists. But with the exception of the French *enfant terrible* Rimbaud, no other writer sensed the coming linguistic revolution—one of tenor rather than felicity. In Nietzsche's prose you can hear the coming voice of the twentieth century: this is the language of the future.

But all this didn't happen at once. When Nietzsche wrote *Human, All Too Human* he was only beginning to find his voice. Even his ideas had in many cases yet to find their mark. This work is filled with an amazing range of psychological aperçus. "The fantasist denies reality to himself, the liar does so only to others." "The mother of excess is not joy but joylessness." "All poets and writers enamored of the superlative want to do more than they can." "A witticism is an epigram on the death of a feeling." But in the end it all becomes too much. His admirers objected that he wasn't writing philosophy, and they were right. This is psychology (though of such quality that a few decades later Freud soon decided against reading any more Nietzsche— for fear he might discover there was nothing left to say on the subject). But the mixture of aphorisms and psychology doesn't make for a coherent extended work. Beneath the psychological aperçus there was little underlying train of argument to link the aphorisms. So Nietzsche's work was branded as unsystematic. It was never to lose this tag—which is unfair. Because of his aphoristic style, he may have appeared unsystematic. But his ideas are as coherent and closely argued as those confined within any of the great philosophic systems.

Yet of course he was unsystematic in the sense that his philosophy spelled the end of all systems. Or should have—but there's always someone willing to have a try. (At precisely this time Karl Marx was hard at work in the British Museum.)

Despite its flaws, *Human, All Too Human* marks Nietzsche's emergence as the finest psychologist of his age. Some feat, considering his lack of social experience. He was essentially a solitary bird. In the normally accepted sense, he scarcely knew anyone. He had no real friends. Throughout his life he retained a few close admirers, but his self-obsession prevented him from entering into the give and take of true friendship. So how did he acquire such profound psychological knowledge? Many commentators are of the opinion that Nietzsche's source in this sphere was just one man—Richard Wagner. This is quite possible. Here indeed was a rich seam of psychological oddity to be mined. But such commentators tend to overlook the fact that Nietzsche also knew himself pretty well (if intermittently, and often a little selectively).

Nietzsche's psychological insights are of universal application despite their eclectic sources—a misanthropic philosopher and a megalomaniac composer. Yet Nietzsche's access to his main psychological source was coming to an end. After the publication of *Human, All Too Human*, the break with Wagner became inevitable. The world for which Nietzsche was preparing in this work was the Brave New World of the future—meanwhile Wagner was now embarking upon his final work, *Parsifal*, which signaled the end of his involvement with Schopenhauer and his return to the fold of Christianity. Their ways had parted forever. It is said that Nietzsche knew only one man properly throughout his entire life, and this man provided him with enough material to become the greatest psychologist of his age. Such was Wagner.

In 1879 Nietzsche was forced to resign his post at Basel because of continuing illness. For years his health had been frail, and now he was a very sick man. He was granted a small pension and advised to take up residence in a more clement climate.

For the next ten years Nietzsche roamed Italy, the south of France, and Switzerland, constantly seeking a climate that would alleviate his illnesses. What was wrong with him? Just about everything, it seems. His eyesight had failed to the point where he was half-blind (the doctor advised him to give up reading; he might as well have recommended that he give up breathing). He suffered from violent incapacitating headaches which would sometimes confine him to bed for days on end, and he was generally a mass of physical ailments and complaints. His desktop collection of elixirs, medicaments, pills, tonics, powders, and potions put him in a class of his own, even among the great hypochondriacal philosophers. Yet this was the man who conceived the idea of the superman. The element of psychological compensation in this idea should not detract from its central place among Nietzsche's other more acceptable ideas. Perhaps such an element was just the grit in the oyster that produced this pearl of unwisdom.

The superman made his appearance in *Thus Spake Zarathustra*, a long "dithyrambic" poem of almost unbearable bombast and earnestness, whose utter humorlessness is unrelieved by its author's attempts at "irony" and leaden "lightness." Like Dostoevsky and Hesse, it's unreadable unless you're a teenager—but the experience of this work at such an age can often "change your life." And not always for the worse. The stupid ideas are easily spottable, and the rest make a challenging antidote to many accepted notions, requiring one to think deeply for oneself. The philosophy, as such, is almost negligible. But the exhortations to philosophy—to think for oneself—are powerful, as are the characterizations of our condition. "Is there such a thing as up and down any more? Are we not

34

drifting through infinite nothingness? . . . Surely
ever deeper night is closing around us? Don't we
need lanterns in the morning? Are we still deaf
to the sound of the grave-diggers digging God's
grave? Can't we smell the stench of divine putre-
faction? . . . The most holy and mighty thing in
the world bled to death under our knives.
. . . No greater deed has ever been done, and
thanks to this deed whoever comes after us will
live in a higher history than there has ever been."
Almost a century later the French existentialists
began expressing such thoughts—in rather less
boisterous terms—and were hailed as the van-
guard of modern thought.

On his endless tour of the spas and mild-
winter resorts, Nietzsche was now introduced by
his friend Paul Rée to a twenty-one-year-old
Russian woman called Lou Salomé. Rée and
Nietzsche (separately and together) would take
her for long walks, and tried to fill her head with
their ideas on philosophy. (Zarathustra was introduced to Lou as "the son I will never have,"
which was fortunate for young Zarathustra, and
not just because of the attention his name might

have attracted in the school playground.) Lou, Nietzsche, and Rée now became involved in a triangular arrangement that would be inconceivable in an age where anyone has even an iota of sexual *savoir-faire*. At first the three of them declared they would all study philosophy and live together in a platonic *ménage à trois*. Then Rée and Nietzsche both (separately) declared they were in love with Lou and decided to propose to her. Unfortunately Nietzsche made the ludicrous mistake of asking Rée to convey his proposal to Lou for him. (This does not invalidate Nietzsche's claim to being the greatest psychologist of his age, as anyone who has become involved in the love life of a psychologist will tell you.) Precisely who was in control of this situation is best demonstrated by a posed photograph of the three of them, taken in a studio in Lucerne. The two emotional virgins (aged thirty-eight and thirty-three) are harnessed to a cart, in which sits the twenty-one-year-old genuine virgin brandishing a whip. In the end the three of them found themselves unable to maintain this high farce any longer, and they split up. Nietzsche was so distraught that he wrote: "This evening I'll take enough opium to send me insane," but eventually he decided that Lou was unworthy to be either the mother or the sister of baby Zarathustra. (Lou went on to become one of the most remarkable women of her age. After adopting the name Andreas-Salomé from her pet husband, a German professor, she was to have a profound effect on two other leading figures of her time—having an influential affair with the great German lyric poet Rilke, and developing an intimate friendship with the aging Freud.)

After wintering in Nice, Turin, Rome, or Menton, Nietzsche would spend his summers "1,500 meters above the world and even higher above all human beings" in Sils Maria, a lakeside hamlet in the Swiss Engadine. Sils Maria is now a smart little resort (just seven miles down the road from St. Moritz), but you can still see the simple room where Nietzsche used to stay and set up his medicine chest. Here the mountains rise sheer from the lakeshore toward the snowcapped 13,000-foot peak of Mount Bernina, which marks the Italian border. Behind the house you can take the remote paths up the mountainsides where Nietzsche used to walk and think out his philosophy, pausing to jot down his conclusions in his notebook beside a lonely crag or a foaming mountain torrent. Some of the atmosphere of this region—the remote peaks, the sweeping views, the sense of isolated grandeur—creeps into the tone of his writings. When you see where Nietzsche did so much of his thinking, some of its faults and virtues become more explicable.

For the most part Nietzsche lived a life of utter isolation, renting inexpensive rooms, working continuously, and eating in cheap restaurants—while doctoring his blinding headaches and debilitating ailments as best he could. It was not unusual for him to spend entire nights retching, and he was frequently incapacitated for three or four days in a week. What's more, this rapidly became a permanent state of affairs. Yet each year he produced a book of astonishing quality. Such works as *The Dawn*, *The Joyful Wisdom*, and *Beyond Good and Evil* contain superb critiques of Western civilization, its values and its psychology as well as its hang-ups. His style is clear and aphoristic, and contains a minimum of loony ideas. This is not systematic philosophy but philosophizing of the highest order. Many (indeed most) of the fundamental values of Western man and Western civilization were tested and found wanting. As he expressed it in his unpublished notebook: "Christianity comes to an end—destroyed by its own morality (which cannot be replaced), a morality which in the end is forced to deny even the existence of its own God. The sense of truthfulness, so highly developed by Christianity, becomes sickened by the falsehoods and mendacity of all Christian interpretations of the world and of history. It rebounds from 'God is truth' to 'All is false.'" There has been no finer demolition job—though much of the purely philosophical demolition work had already been done over a century earlier by Hume. (But it needed to be done again because of the resurgence of German metaphysical systems.)

Throughout the 1880s Nietzsche continued to work on in solitude, unknown and unread, gradually driving himself ever harder as he found his utter solitude and lack of recognition ever more unbearable. Then in 1888 the Danish Jewish scholar Georg Brandes began delivering lectures on Nietzsche's philosophy at the University of Copenhagen. By then it was unfortunately too late. In 1888 Nietzsche finished no less than four books, and the cracks were beginning to show. His was a great mind and he knew it: it was imperative that the world should know this too. In *Ecce Homo* he describes *Thus Spake Zarathustra* as "the highest and deepest book in existence"—a statement which stretches critical altimeters and credulity alike. As if this isn't enough, there follow chapters headed "Why I Am So Wise," "Why I Write Such Great Books," and "Why I Am Destiny," in which he advises against alcohol, endorses oilless cocoa, and commends his bowel habits. The bombast and self-absorption of *Zarathustra* were reappearing with a vengeance—in mania.

In January 1889 the end came. While walking down a street in Turin he collapsed, flinging his arms tearfully around the neck of a horse which had just been whipped by its driver. Nietzsche was assisted to his room where he wrote postcards to Cosima Wagner ("I love you, Ariadne"), the king of Italy ("My beloved Umberto ... I am having all anti-Semites shot"), and to Jacob Burckhardt (signing himself "Dionysius"). Burckhardt understood what had happened and passed the card on to a friend of Nietzsche's, who went at once to collect him.

Nietzsche was now clinically insane, and never recovered. Almost certainly his condition would have been incurable even today. It was brought on by overwork, solitude, and suffering—but the prime cause was syphilis. This had reached the tertiary stage, which apparently involves "mental paralysis." After a brief spell in an asylum, Nietzsche was released into the care of his mother. He was now harmless, existing for much of the time in a catatonic trance which reduced him to an almost vegetal state. During his more lucid moments he appeared to have a vague memory of his past life. When he was handed a book he remarked, "Didn't I write good books, too?"

After Nietzsche's mother died in 1897, he was looked after by his sister Elisabeth Förster-Nietzsche. This was the last person who should have been put in charge of him. Nietzsche's younger sister Elisabeth had married Bernard Förster, a failed schoolmaster who became a notorious anti-Semite. Nietzsche despised him both as a man and for his ideas. Förster had set up an Aryan race colony called Nueva Germania in Paraguay, using poor yeoman farmers from Saxony. He ended up defrauding them and then committed suicide. (The remnants of Nueva Germania still exist in Paraguay, where the "master race" now live much the same as the local Indians, virtually indistinguishable except for their blond hair.) When Elisabeth returned to Germany and took charge of her insane brother, she was determined to turn him into a great figure. She moved him to Weimar because of its elevated cultural associations with Goethe and Schiller, with the aim of establishing a Nietzsche archive. Then she began doctoring her brother's unpublished notebooks, inserting anti-Semitic ideas and flattering remarks about herself. These notebooks were published as *The Will to Power*, which has since been purged of this rubbish by the great Nietzsche scholar Walter Kaufmann, to produce what is arguably Nietzsche's greatest work.

At the outset Nietzsche states the condition of the coming age: "Skepticism about morality is what is decisive. The ending of the moral interpretation of the world, which no longer has any sanction after it has tried to escape into some metaphysical beyond, leads to nihilism. 'Everything lacks meaning' (the untenability of [the Christian] interpretation of the world, upon which such a huge amount of energy has been lavished, awakens the suspicion that *all* interpretations of the world are false)." This may appear to render all philosophy superfluous, but Nietzsche continues gamely nonetheless: "The entire apparatus of knowledge is an apparatus for abstraction and simplification—directed not at knowledge, but at taking possession of things: 'end' and 'means' are as remote from its essential nature as are 'concepts.'" He goes on to show what our knowledge is: "All our organs of knowledge and our senses are developed only as a means of preservation and growth. Trust in reason and its categories, in dialectic, therefore the valuation of logic, proves only their usefulness for life, proved by experience—not that something is true." His psychological remarks remain as perceptive as ever, but now these lead from aperçus to fundamental (and dangerous) insights. "Pleasure appears where there is the feeling of power. Happiness lies in the triumphant consciousness of power and victory. Progress lies in the strengthening of the type, the aptitude for strong use of the will. Everything else is a dangerous misunderstanding."

Nietzsche eventually made it into the twentieth century, whose nature he had predicted so well. A pathetic pale little figure with an enormous military mustache, who had little idea of who or where he was, he finally died August 25, 1900.

Afterword

Nietzsche died two deaths. His mind died in 1889, his body in 1900. Between these dates his work took on a life of its own, launching Nietzsche from almost total obscurity to worldwide intellectual eminence. Nietzsche would of course have considered this no more than his due. But this fame was to exceed even his own megalomaniacal fantasies. It extended far beyond the field of philosophy, largely owing to Nietzsche's appeal to writers. The list of major twentieth-century figures Nietzsche influenced includes Yeats, Strindberg, O'Neill, Shaw, Rilke, Mann, Conrad, Freud, and countless lesser figures who were simply overwhelmed by his ideas. This was a philosophy with a difference: one with style and lucidity. Here was a philosophy you could actually read. And the fact that it was written in aphorisms meant you also had time to read it (or bits of it).

And this was the trouble. Now lots of people read just bits of Nietzsche. Such ideas as the Will to Power and the Superman became commonplace and widely misused. Nietzsche's superman was soon hijacked by the racist lobby. Anti-Semites, then fascists, began lifting remarks from Nietzsche's work, regardless of context. The very looseness of Nietzsche's philosophy now became its undoing.

As a result of its grotesque misuse during the first half of the twentieth century, Nietzsche's philosophy was badly discredited. Consequently it is almost impossible to talk about many of Nietzsche's ideas in the way he intended (especially his ideas about the superman, "discipline," "breeding," and the like). The poetic looseness of much of his writing left it too open to hideous travesty. Fortunately it also left his remarks on such dangerous topics open to ridicule, which is perhaps the most appropriate contemporary response. Yet it is worth remembering that Nietzsche made his views on racism, anti-Semitism, and related attitudes perfectly plain. As he clearly states: "The homogenizing of European man is the greatest process that cannot be obstructed: one should even hasten it." When the Nazis attempted to take him on board as their official philosopher, and Hitler kissed Elisabeth Förster-Nietzsche's hand outside the Nietzsche Archiv in Weimar, it was the Nazis who entered the realms of higher lunacy, not Nietzsche's philosophy.

Nietzsche's Key Philosophical Concepts

Nietzsche's philosophy was written mainly in aphorisms and is not methodical. His attitude remains largely consistent, but his thought is constantly developing in different directions. This means that he frequently appears to contradict himself, or leaves himself open to conflicting interpretations. His was a philosophy of penetrating insights, not a system. Yet certain words and concepts recur again and again in his work. In these the elements of a system are detectable.

The Will to Power

This is the major concept in Nietzsche's philosophy. He developed it from two main sources: Schopenhauer and the ancient Greeks. Schopenhauer had adopted the oriental idea that the universe was driven by a vast blind will. Nietzsche recognized the force of this idea and adapted it to human terms. In the course of Nietzsche's studies of the ancient Greeks, he concluded that the driving force of their civilization had been the search for power rather than anything useful or immediately beneficial.

Nietzsche concluded that humanity was driven by a Will to Power. The basic impulse for all our acts could be traced back to this one source. Often it became transformed from its primary expression, or even perverted, but it was always there. Christianity appeared to preach the very opposite, with its ideas of humility, brotherly love, and compassion. But in fact this was no more than a subtle perversion of the Will to Power. Christianity was a religion born out of slavery in the Roman era, and it had never lost its slave mentality. This was the Will to Power of slaves rather than the more recognizable Will to Power of the powerful.

Nietzsche's Will to Power proved a very useful tool when he came to analyzing human motive. Acts which had previously appeared noble or honorably disinterested were now often revealed as decadent or sick.

But Nietzsche failed to answer two main objections. If the Will to Power was the only yardstick, how could actions that appeared not to follow its immediate dictates be other than degenerate or perverted? Take, for instance, the life of a saint or an ascetic philosopher such as Spinoza (whom Nietzsche admired). To say that the saint or ascetic philosopher was exercising his Will to Power on himself was surely to render the concept so flexible as to be almost meaningless. Second, Nietzsche's notion of the Will to Power was circular: if our attempt to understand the universe was inspired by the Will to Power, surely the concept of the Will to Power was inspired by Nietzsche's attempt to understand the universe.

51

But the last word on this penetrating but dangerous concept should remain Nietzsche's: "The manner of this lust for power has changed through the centuries, but its source is still the same volcano. . . . What we once did 'for the sake of God' we now do for the sake of money. . . . This is what at present gives the highest feeling of power" [*Die Morgenrote (The Dawn)*, 204].

Eternal Recurrence

According to Nietzsche, we should act as if the life we are living will go on recurring forever. Each moment we have lived through we will have to relive again and again for eternity.

This is essentially a metaphysical moral fable. But Nietzsche insisted on treating it as if he believed in it. He described it as his "formula for the greatness of a human being."

This supreme and impossibly romantic stress on the importance of the moment is intended as an exhortation to live our lives to the full. As a passing poetic idea, it has some force. As a philosophical or moral idea, it is essentially superficial. It simply doesn't bear thinking through. The cliché "Live life to the full" at least means something, however vague. The idea of eternal recurrence turns out on inspection to be meaningless. Do we remember each of these recurring lives? If we do, we would surely make changes. If we don't, they are of no relevance. Even an arresting poetic image—and this is one—must have more substance if it is to be regarded as more than mere poetry. It is simply too nebulous to be used as a principle, as Nietzsche intended.

The Superman

Nietzsche's superman had nothing whatsoever to do with the cloaked figure who flies through the skies of comic books. It might have been better if Nietzsche's hero had adopted a few of his namesake's comic values. Clark Kent at least has a naive morality, which he attempts to impose on a rough-and-ready world of good guys and bad guys. Nietzsche's superman had no truck with such constraints as morality. His only "morality" was the Will to Power. Yet curiously, Nietzsche's descriptions of his superman show him inhabiting a world as filled with naive simplicities as any comic.

The prototype for Nietzsche's superman was his Zarathustra—an impossibly earnest and boring fellow, whose behavior exhibited dangerous psychotic symptoms. Admittedly the tale of Zarathustra was intended as a parable. But a parable of what? As a parable of behavior. The parables that Christ preached in the Sermon on the Mount appear childishly simple—but on reflection are neither childish nor simple. They are profound. The parable of Zarathustra is childishly simple, and on reflection remains so. Yet its message is profound, despite this. Nietzsche preaches nothing less than the overthrow of Christian values: each individual must take absolute responsibility for his own actions in a godless world. He must make his own values in unfettered freedom. There is no sanction, divine or otherwise, for his actions. Nietzsche foresaw this as the twentieth-century condition. Unfortunately he also made prescriptions as to how we should behave in this condition. Those who followed his prescriptions (the tedious antics of Zarathustra) would become supermen.

Alas, Nietzsche's superman was to develop into more than the figure of comic fun that he so richly deserved to become. In *Thus Spake Zarathustra*, Nietzsche announces (through the mouth of his hero): "What is the ape to man? A figure of fun or an embarrassment. Man will appear exactly the same to the superman" [*Thus Spake Zarathustra*, First Part, Zarathustra's Prologue, Part 3]. Elsewhere he proclaims: "The goal of humanity cannot lie in its end but in its highest specimens" [*Genealogy of Morals*, 2nd Meditation, Section 9]. In this context he begins loosely and misguidedly linking the superman to such notions as "nobility" and "blood." But he was not talking in aristocratic racial terms. He refers at one point to "the Almanac de Gotha: an enclosure for asses" [*Will to Power*, 942—revised edition 1906 or 1911; in the Härtle edition this remark has been left out, without indication] and announces on another occasion, "When I speak of Plato, Pascal, Spinoza, and Goethe, then I know their blood rolls in mine" [Musarion Edition (1920–1929) of *Collected Works*, XXI, 98]. A Greek, a Frenchman, a Portuguese Jew, and a German—all blood ancestors of the superman, in Nietzsche's view.

From Nietzsche's Writings

Aphorisms and Catchphrases

God is Dead.

Live dangerously.

What is the best remedy? Victory.
—*The Dawn*, 571

There are no moral phenomena at all, only moral interpretations of phenomena. . . .
—*Beyond Good and Evil*, 108

The best cure for love is still that time-honored medicine: love returned.
—*The Dawn*, Book IV, 415

Convictions are more hazardous enemies of truth than lies.
—*Human, All Too Human*, Vol I, Sec 9, 483

People who understand a thing to its very depths seldom remain faithful to it forever. For they have brought these depths into clear daylight; and what is in the depths is not usually pleasant to see.
—*Human, All Too Human*, 489

Even the bravest only rarely have the courage for what they really know.
—*Twilight of the Idols*, Maxims and Arrows, 2

Here Nietzsche is so fearless that he shows he is not even afraid of being hoist on his own petard:

Public opinions, private idleness.

Philosophizing

As an example of the sheer quality of Nietzsche's sustained philosophizing, here he takes apart our notion of truth and what it means (using a flawlessly "true" argument in the process). He arrives at a number of original insights en route, some of which are particularly timely in view of what we have done, and are continuing to do, to ourselves and the planet in the name of science. The implications of his argument remain as devastating now as they were then.

What is this unconditional will to truth? . . . What do you know from the outset of the character of existence, which can enable us to decide whether it is best to be on the side of the unconditionally mistrustful or of the unconditionally trusting? Yet if both are required, much trust and mistrust: from where can science take its unconditional faith, the conviction on which it rests, that truth is more important than anything else, even than any other conviction? This conviction could not have come into being if both truth and untruth showed themselves to be continually useful, as is the case. So although there undeniably exists a faith in science, it cannot derive from such a utilitarian calculus but must instead have originated in spite of the fact that the inutility and the dangerousness of the "will to truth," of "truth at any price" are proved to it continually. . . .

Therefore "will to truth" does not mean "I will not let myself be deceived" but there is no alternative "I will not deceive, not even myself": and here we are on the ground of morality. We must ask ourselves carefully: "Why don't we want to deceive?" especially if it appears—and it certainly does appear—that life depends on appearance: I mean, on error, falsehood, deception, self-deception; and where life has, in fact, always shown itself to be on the side of the most unscrupulous multiplicity. Such an intent, inter-

60

preted charitably, could possibly be a quixotism, a degree of enthusiastic impudence; but it could also be something worse, namely, a destructive principle, hostile to life. "Will to truth"—this could be a concealed will to death.

So the question "Why science?" leads back to the moral problem. "Why is there any morality at all?" if life, nature, and history are "not moral"? . . . Yet you will have understood by now what I am driving at, namely, that it always remains a metaphysical faith upon which our faith in science rests that even we modern scholars, we godless ones and antimetaphysicians, still kindle our fire too from the flame which a faith thousands of years old has kindled: that Christian faith, which was also Plato's faith, that God is truth, that truth is divine. . . .

—*Gay Science*, Book V, Sec 344

A related argument, only apparently contradicting the above, explains the demise of Christianity:

Christianity comes to an end destroyed by its own morality (which cannot be replaced), a morality which in the end is forced to deny even the existence of its own God. The sense of truthfulness, so highly developed by Christianity, becomes sickened by the falsehoods and mendacity of all Christian interpretations of the world and of history. It rebounds from "God is truth" to the fanatical faith "All is false."

—*Will to Power*, Book 1, Introduction

One of Nietzsche's more sober prescriptions for superhumanity, and in many ways one of his more revealing:

What makes heroic? To confront simultaneously one's greatest sorrow and one's greatest hope.

What do you believe in? I believe that the weight of all things must be determined anew.

What does your conscience tell you? "You must become who you are."

Where is your greatest danger? In pity.

What do you love in others? My hopes.

62

Whom do you call bad? He who always desires to make one ashamed.

What is for you the most humane thing? To spare someone shame.

What is the seal of freedom attained? No longer to be ashamed of oneself.

—*Gay Science*, 268, 275

Thinking Dangerously

In all writing I love only what is written with blood. Write with blood: and you discover that blood is spirit. . . .

I want gremlins around me, for I am courageous. Courage frightens away specters and creates gremlins for itself. Courage wants to laugh.

I no longer feel as you do: this cloud which I see beneath me, this darkness and heaviness which I laugh at, precisely this is your thundercloud.

You look up when you desire to be exalted. I look down because I am exalted.

Who among you can simultaneously laugh and be exalted?

He who climbs upon the highest mountains laughs at all tragedies, real or imaginary.

Courageous, unperturbed, mocking, violent—this is what wisdom wants to be: wisdom is a woman and loves only a warrior.

—Thus Spake Zarathustra I,
Of Reading and Writing

"Man is evil"—all the wisest men have told me that to comfort me. Oh, if only this were true today! For evil is man's strength.

"Man must grow better and more evil"—this is what I teach. The greatest evil is necessary for the superman's greatest achievement.

Perhaps it was good the poor peoples' sage took upon himself and suffered the sins of humanity. I, on the other hand, rejoice in great sins as my consolation. . . .

—Thus Spake Zarathustra IV,
Of the Higher Man, 5

The superman Zarathustra hymns the joys of solitary ardor and the prospect of being able to do it all over again ("the ring of the return" refers to Nietzsche's doctrine of Eternal Recurrence, which proposes that our lives are repeated over and over again forever). Needless to say, this unwittingly hilarious piece of self-exposure was written with a pre-Freudian audience in mind.

I have drunk a bowl filled with foaming spice and one in which everthing is well mixed:

My hand has gone back and forth, mingling fire with spirit, joy with sorrow, and the hardest with the softest:

I have become a grain of the saving salt which makes everything in the bowl mix well:

For there is a salt which blends good and evil; and even the most evil thing is worthy, as it adds spice and makes everything spill over in a froth:

Ah, how could I not be ardent for Eternity, and for the marriage ring of rings the ring of the return?

I have never yet found a woman with whom I should like to have children, unless it be this woman whom I love: for I love thee, O Eternity! For I love thee, O Eternity!

—*Thus Spake Zarathustra* LX,
The Seven Seals, 4

When he descends from such lofty regions (and language), Nietzsche demonstrates that he is capable of the most succinct and penetrating arguments:

The "thing-in-itself" is a nonsensical concept. If I remove all the relationships, all the "properties," all the "activities" of a thing, nothing remains. Thingness has only been invented by us to fit the requirements of logic. In other words, with the aim of defining, of communication. (In order to bind together the multiplicity of relationships, properties, and activities.)

—*Will to Power*, 558

"Truth": according to my way of thinking, this doesn't necessarily mean the antithesis of error but in the more fundamental cases only the posture of various errors in relation to one another. Perhaps one is older, more profound than another, even ineradicable, in so far as the organic entity of our species could not live without it. Other errors do not tyrannize us as conditions of life in quite this way, but on the contrary when compared with such "tyrants" can be set aside and "refuted."

An assumption that is irrefutable—why should it for that reason be "true"? This proposition may well outrage logicians, who posit their limitations as the limitations of things. But long ago I declared war on this optimism of logicians.

—*Will to Power*, 535

Astonishingly, in light of his attacks on Christianity, Nietzsche also asserts:

67

The continuance of the Christian ideal is a most desirable thing—even for those ideals that want to stand beside it and perhaps above it—they must have opponents, strong opponents, if they are themselves to become strong.

—*Will to Power*, 361

And a final word of warning:

Beware of syphilitics preaching morals.

—Saul Bellow, *Herzog*

Chronology of Significant Philosophical Dates

6th C B.C.	The beginning of Western philosophy with Thales of Miletus.
End of 6th C B.C.	Death of Pythagoras.
399 B.C.	Socrates sentenced to death in Athens.
c 387 B.C.	Plato founds the Academy in Athens, the first university.
335 B.C.	Aristotle founds the Lyceum in Athens, a rival school to the Academy.

324 A.D.	Emperor Constantine moves capital of Roman Empire to Byzantium.
400 A.D.	St. Augustine writes his *Confessions*. Philosophy absorbed into Christian theology.
410 A.D.	Sack of Rome by Visigoths heralds opening of Dark Ages.
529 A.D.	Closure of Academy in Athens by Emperor Justinian marks end of Hellenic thought.
Mid-13th C	Thomas Aquinas writes his commentaries on Aristotle. Era of Scholasticism.
1453	Fall of Byzantium to Turks, end of Byzantine Empire.
1492	Columbus reaches America. Renaissance in Florence and revival of interest in Greek learning.
1543	Copernicus publishes *On the Revolution of the Celestial Orbs*, proving mathematically that the earth revolves around the sun.

1633	Galileo forced by church to recant heliocentric theory of the universe.
1641	Descartes publishes his *Meditations*, the start of modern philosophy.
1677	Death of Spinoza allows publication of his *Ethics*.
1687	Newton publishes *Principia*, introducing concept of gravity.
1689	Locke publishes *Essay Concerning Human Understanding*. Start of empiricism.
1710	Berkeley publishes *Principles of Human Knowledge*, advancing empiricism to new extremes.
1716	Death of Leibniz.
1739–1740	Hume publishes *Treatise of Human Nature*, taking empiricism to its logical limits.
1781	Kant, awakened from his "dogmatic slumbers" by Hume, publishes *Critique of Pure Reason*.

Great era of German metaphysics begins.

1807 Hegel publishes *The Phenomenology of Mind*, high point of German metaphysics.

1818 Schopenhauer publishes *The World as Will and Representation*, introducing Indian philosophy into German metaphysics.

1889 Nietzsche, having declared "God is dead," succumbs to madness in Turin.

1921 Wittgenstein publishes *Tractatus Logico-Philosophicus*, claiming the "final solution" to the problems of philosophy.

1920s Vienna Circle propounds Logical Positivism.

1927 Heidegger publishes *Being and Time*, heralding split between analytical and Continental philosophy.

1943 Sartre publishes *Being and Nothingness*, advancing

72

Heidegger's thought and instigating existentialism.

1953   Posthumous publication of Wittgenstein's *Philosophical Investigations*. High era of linguistic analysis.

Chronology of Nietzsche's Life

October 15, 1844	Friedrich Wilhelm Nietzsche born at Röcken in Saxony, Germany.
1849	Death of Nietzsche's father.
1850	Nietzsche's mother moves the family to Naumburg.
1858	Nietzsche enters boarding school at Pforta.
1864	Studies at Bonn University.
1865	Moves to Leipzig University.
1868	First meeting with Wagner.

1869	Takes up post at University of Basel, in Switzerland.
1871	Publishes *Birth of Tragedy*.
1878	Publishes *Human, All Too Human*.
1882	Becomes involved with Rée in fiasco over Lou Salomé.
1883	Publishes first parts of *Thus Spake Zarathustra*.
1889	Suffers irreversible mental collapse on a street in Turin.
1900	Death in Weimar after over a decade in a catatonic trance.

Chronology of Nietzsche's Era

1850	Schopenhauer publishes *Essays, Aphorisms, and Maxims*, the work that was to bring him belatedly to public notice.
1853–1856	Crimean War.
1856	Birth of Freud.
1860	Burckhardt publishes *The Civilization of the Renaissance in Italy*. Death of Schopenhauer.
1861–1865	American Civil War.
1865	First performance of Wagner's *Tristan and Isolde*.
1870–1871	Franco-Prussian War alters

	balance of power in Europe in favor of Germans.
1875	First performance of Bizet's opera *Carmen*.
1876	Opening of Bayreuth Opera House for performance of works by Wagner.
1882	First performance of Wagner's *Parsifal*.
1883	Death of Wagner.
1889	Birth of Wittgenstein.
1896	Klondike gold rush.
1900	Freud publishes *Interpretation of Dreams*.

Recommended Reading

Arthur C. Danto, *Nietzsche as Philosopher* (Columbia University Press, 1980)

Ronald Hayman, *Nietzsche* (Penguin, 1993)

Walter Kaufmann, ed., *The Portable Nietzsche* (Viking, 1977)

F. A. Lea, *The Tragic Philosopher: Friedrich Nietzsche* (Athlone, 1993)

Alexander Nehamas, *Nietzsche: Life as Literature* (Harvard University Press, 1985)

Index

A NOTE ON THE AUTHOR

Paul Strathern has lectured in philosophy and mathematics and now lives and writes in London. A Somerset Maugham prize winner, he is also the author of books on history and travel as well as five novels. His articles have appeared in a great many publications, including the *Observer* (London) and the *Irish Times.* His own degree in philosophy was earned at Trinity College, Dublin.

NOW PUBLISHED IN THIS SERIES:

Plato in 90 Minutes
Aristotle in 90 Minutes
Descartes in 90 Minutes
Kant in 90 Minutes
Nietzsche in 90 Minutes
Wittgenstein in 90 Minutes

IN PREPARATION:

Thomas Aquinas, Saint Augustine, Bacon,
Berkeley, Confucius, Hegel, Hume,
Kierkegaard, Leibniz, Locke, Machiavelli,
Marx, J. S. Mill, Bertrand Russell, Sartre,
Schopenhauer, Socrates, Spinoza